How to Interview

What Employers Want to Hear
in Today's Competitive Job Market

RUSS HOVENDICK

Faithful Life Publishers & Printers
North Fort Myers, FL 33903

FaithfulLifePublishers.com

ISBN: 978-1-937129-66-8

Directional Motivation, LLC.
5421 W 41st #202
Sioux Falls, SD 57106

(605) 362-8176 ext 101

www.DirectionalMotivation.com
russ@directionalmotivation.com

Published and printed by:
Faithful Life Publishers & Printers
3335 Galaxy Way
North Fort Myers, FL 33903

(888)720-0950

www.FaithfulLifePublishers.com
info@FaithfulLifePublishers.com

19 18 17 16 15 14 13   1 2 3 4 5

ACKNOWLEDGMENTS

This book required a tremendous amount of input and assistance from many individuals. To those HR professionals who allowed my quick questions to evolve into hour-long conversations, thank you for being so generous with your time and sharing your insights. They were spot-on. To my wife, who supported me while I spent hours on end in front of the computer, I could not have done this without you. I would be remiss not to thank the following members of the Directional Motivation team: Millie Lapidario for once again helping me construct my thoughts, Molly Meester for creating vibrant images to capture the thoughts behind this book, and Darin, my son, who has the unwanted task of keeping me focused on one project at a time. Anyone who knows me understands that this task is nearly impossible. Darin, you did a great job, and I hope you still love me after all that I put you through. I could not be more proud.

FOREWORD

If you are ready to take the next step in your career, this book will prove to be one of your most valuable resources. I make this bold statement with the utmost confidence that it will help job seekers from all walks of life, including recent graduates, military veterans, those who've been fired or laid off, and stay-at-home moms ready to go back to work. As a Fortune 500 human resource professional with over twenty years of industry experience, I can assure you: this resource will not only enhance your interview skills, it will also systematically improve your overall communication.

Russ Hovendick, author of the Directional Motivation books, has once again put his signature touch on this instruction manual by challenging individuals to self-evaluate and truly know themselves before they enter the interview room. He breaks down complex interview techniques in a way that empowers readers to understand and start using them right away. The wisdom he shares in this manuscript is classic. And by offering additional online worksheets and tools, he has created a winning package for any job seeker.

I am a huge fan!

Best regards / Mit freundlichen Grüßen

BLG Logistics, Inc.

Zina Cooper, PHR
Director of Human Resources

BOOK REVIEWS

"For years, I've been pushing my friend Russ Hovendick, an executive recruiter, to put his wealth of real world knowledge into book form. No one knows communication and advancement in the workplace better than Russ. Finally, he's delivered! His first book, *How to Get a Raise*, gave easy-to-follow steps for navigating the difficult waters of the pay raise request. Now, the second book in his Directional Motivation series has arrived. In *How to Interview: What Employers Want to Hear in Today's Competitive Job Market*, Russ has compiled an insider's guide to succeeding in that simple conversation—"the interview"—that seems to stymie so many people. Russ breaks down the stigma and nerves surrounding an interview to show the basic transaction taking place between two parties who only want to benefit from the exchange. I encourage aspiring applicants across all fields to read what Russ has to say before stepping into the interview room. You will thank yourself at the closing handshake."

Janine Harvey, Owner
Executive Search and Placement

"Executive Recruiter Russ Hovendick reframes the job interview power dynamic in a clear, concise strategy through nuts-and-bolts wisdom. It's easy to find yourself overwhelmed by the interrogating eye, but by applying the simple principles in this book, you'll actually find yourself embracing it. Now you control your own destiny with clarity and control."

Christopher Vondracek, English Instructor
Saint Mary's University of Minnesota

"The world of hiring is full of pat responses—*hard worker, people person, never misses a deadline.* But do these words actually work for or against you? In *How to Interview: What Employers Want to Hear in Today's Competitive Job Market*, Russ Hovendick dispels common wisdom, shunning buzz phraseology and instead, shows readers how to harness the power of storytelling to strengthen their interviews. Even the most seasoned candidates will benefit from the language games and reflective exercises Russ peppers throughout this book."

Jeff Cundick, Senior Director of Operations
Fortune 500 Company

"As an educator for over 25 years, I have scoured the shelves for resources that would challenge and make a lasting imprint on my students. *How to Interview: What Employers Want to Hear in Today's Competitive Job Market* is exactly what I needed for my Workplace Readiness class. This book provides so much more than the name implies. It teaches communication and presentation skills that so many of our young people are lacking. From the moment I picked up this book, I couldn't stop reading it. High school students of all levels will be able to grasp the concepts because of the book's easily understandable, conversational writing style. I'm definitely adding this to my curriculum. In fact, this should be a required read for every student prior to graduating from high school."

Jan Meester, High School Teacher

"True to the abilities of a great teacher, Russ Hovendick offers a hands-on approach to coach job seekers through the nerve-racking interview process. His book pinpoints common sense principles backed by real-life examples from his decades of recruiting. *How to Interview: What Employers Want to Hear in Today's Competitive Job Market* is an entertaining and smart must-read for candidates who want to bring their A-game to the interview."

Tammy Mentzer Brown,
Author of *A Teacher's Prayer*
Human Resource Professional

"Wow! This book is a sparkling gem vitally needed by today's job seeker. As a human resource manager, I have read all types of books aimed at helping prospective interviewees improve their interviewing skills. Nothing is as painful as watching candidates struggle to apply difficult or off-base techniques suggested by those resources. In *How to Interview: What Employers Want to Hear in Today's Competitive Job Market,* Russ Hovendick has hit a homerun. He uses a cadre of unique, simple, straightforward exercises to teach readers how to build a solid interviewing foundation, then shows them how to adopt a presentation guaranteed to catch the attention of any employer. If you want to land that job now, this book will deliver. You'll likely turn to it again throughout your entire career."

Robin Ludwikowski, former Human Resource Manager
Fortune 500 Company

TABLE OF CONTENTS

PREFACE

"Tell me about yourself."

If you're like most people, hearing this in a job interview triggers a cold shiver down your spine. Immediately, you ask yourself, "What do I say? Where do I start? Oh man, where do I begin—my childhood? Birth order? Why my mother dressed me differently as a child . . . Who knows?" Once you attempt to answer the question, the second round of panic hits as you observe your interviewer's body language. You continue asking yourself, "Am I getting his attention? Why is he looking at his watch and squirming around in his chair? And why is he suddenly looking at the floor instead of me?"

Has this ever happened to you? As an award-winning executive recruiter for twenty years and an employer myself, I know for a fact that this happens to more people than you would imagine. But it doesn't have to happen to you again. In this book, I will provide a step-by-step plan that will help you successfully present yourself in the best light possible during a job interview.

Do I guarantee that you will be hired? No one can guarantee this, but I assure you that after applying the simple principles in this book, you will be able to approach future interviews with power and confidence. This is a guarantee.

INTRODUCTION
WHY YOU NEED THIS BOOK

If you're a recent college graduate, most likely you borrowed a whopping $25,000–$120,000 to pay for your education. And now, for some odd reason, Old Uncle Sam wants you to pay him back . . . now! With this amount of debt, should you settle for just any job or hold out for your dream job? What's the likelihood of even landing a job in today's rough market?

Sorry, I don't mean to make you panic. You are not alone. In fact, your student loan debt is a minute speck in the nation's total student loan balance of $870 billion reported in 2011 by *U.S. News & World Report*. The same article reports that delinquency rates on student loan debt are nearly twice that of other household debt. Student loan borrowers are having a difficult time paying off loans because of another depressing figure from the U.S. Bureau of Labor Statistics: the 7.7 percent unemployment rate in February 2013.

We all know the competition for jobs among recent grads is fierce. Student loan debt coupled with unemployment or a low-wage job can be a recipe for disaster. To land a top job, you will definitely need to be at the top of your game during a job interview. First impressions are everything. So how do you present yourself as the candidate employers want to hire?

Allow me to help you.

My whole life's purpose has been to help others. I love making a difference in the lives of people and organizations. I mentioned earlier I've spent twenty years as an executive recruiter. I'm also a business owner and twenty-year volunteer chaplain at a prison, jail, and boys juvenile ranch. Through those experiences, I've had the opportunity to counsel and coach individuals from all walks of life, including inmates, the unemployed, hourly workers, recent college graduates, seasoned craftsmen, and top-level executives. In my career, I have also dealt with employers ranging in size from small mom and pop operations up to Fortune 500 companies. As an executive recruiter, career coach, and counselor, it's my job to listen, perceive needs, and recommend tailored solutions.

These days, in my daily conversations with job seekers and employers from a wide variety of industries, I hear that there is a tremendous disconnect during interview sessions. This is what typically happens: Employers ask questions and the candidates answer them. Yet, employers are not getting the information they need, so they continue searching for the "right" person long after they've met many highly skilled and talented job seekers. Meanwhile, the rejected applicants continue to lose their confidence with every unsuccessful interview. By the time they reach out to me for help, they often tell me they don't have the slightest idea of how to better their game. What a shame!

The more I listened and worked with college graduates and other individuals relatively new to the work force, I realized they needed something very specific: an insider's view of the hiring matrix. If more people understood the employer's perspective more intimately, then surely, the interview process wouldn't be so frightening, right? My intention for this book is to offer people in the early stages of their careers, as well seasoned professionals, the lessons I've picked up after twenty years of hearing rants and raves from both the employers and the applicants.

I firmly believe that the little steps you take today will determine your future success. This book is designed specifically to guide you through those steps. I'll provide key insights and exercises to help you present yourself with the power to make the interviewer think, "Wow, this candidate is top-notch. Can't let this one get away!"

Think for a moment: What could landing the ideal job mean to your overall happiness? What would the perfect job mean for your long-term life vision? How could getting the perfect job benefit you financially now and through the next thirty years?

What I'm about to share has the potential to dramatically impact every area of your life. By applying the information in this book, you'll have a fighting chance at building the career and life you want.

CHAPTER 1
THE REAL YOU: YOUR BEST ASSET

I don't care who you are or what you've accomplished so far. I know for a fact that you have something valuable to offer. If you don't have much work experience under your belt, you may have a difficult time identifying what would make an employer want to hire you. I understand that, and I'm here to help you figure that out.

Are you good at showing other people how to do things? If yes, then you are a good leader and communicator. Do people let you borrow money? If yes, then you are trustworthy. Do people ask you for your opinion? If yes, then you must have sound judgment and keen insights. Can you sit through thirty minutes stuck in bumper-to-bumper traffic without going crazy? If yes, then your patience level far exceeds mine!

These character traits are your assets, and they play a significant role in determining your value in the marketplace. If you were going to apply for a loan at the bank, the banker would ask you to identify your assets. If you couldn't provide this information, you'd most likely get rejected. The same is true when you approach an employer. In the employer's mind, you are a potential investment. She is trying to figure out whether spending money on your salary, benefits, and training will give her a return on her investment. You must know what assets only you can bring to a company. Otherwise, the message you'll be sending is, "I don't know what I can do for you, but I'm hoping I'll get lucky and land the job anyway."

Your attributes, along with your education, professional background, and life experience make up your brand. Yes, you are a brand.

Let's take a step back and play a quick game to clarify my point about branding yourself. What is the first thing that comes to mind when you hear "Melts in your mouth, not in your hand"? M&Ms. "Just do it." Nike, of course. "Let's motor." MiniCooper. "Think different." Apple. "Because you're worth it." L'Oréal.

The examples can go on and on. Think of the huge influence these taglines have made on children, athletes, drivers, techies, and women. These companies have developed memorable, feel-good taglines in order to attract new customers and stay on the minds of current and potential customers. Think about it: the employer is a potential customer, as well. The employer is shopping around for the right individual who will fill a position. In order to be chosen, you must have an intimate connection with your brand and be able to present it.

To show you how I've developed my personal brand, here's my Twitter profile description: "I recruit, I write, I change lives." Short, sweet, and to the point. I offer this as a short example to give you an idea of how to craft your brand identity. My Twitter profile statement reflects the image I want to leave people with. When you present yourself at a job interview, your goal is to spark the other person's curiosity. You want all prospective employers to perk up when you begin talking. Ideally, they will prod for more information: "What do you mean?" or "How do you do that?"

Principle No. 1: Employers want to see your heart and passion.

Let's get you in the right mindset to bring out the "real you"—or "best you"—that will delight your interviewer. So we begin the first and most important step of preparing for your interview: self-examination.

There will be several exercises in the upcoming chapters of this book, and I highly recommend that you make the most of them by using the corresponding Directional Motivation worksheets available on our website at www.directionalmotivation.com. You may download and print them from the Resources page.

Warm-up Exercise

Answer the questions below. Consider how the answers define you and how they make you different from others. Also, consider what those answers reflect about your personality, work ethic, and values.

- Did you work while attending college?

- Have you supervised people?

- Were you responsible for money?

- How did you perform in the functions above?

- What comments did you receive from your customers, boss, or coworkers?

- What have you learned from your work experience so far?

- What do your performance evaluations say about you? Why?

• In high school or college, did you belong to or lead any groups? Why did you choose to belong to that group or accept the leadership role? What were you trying to gain from this experience?

• Do others trust you? Why?

• What volunteer activities have you been involved in? Why did you choose these?

If you haven't worked:

• What characteristics have helped you succeed in the past, whether on a team, in a group, or in class?

• What motivates your life decisions?

• When have you failed? What did you learn from those failures?

• Would others describe you as a natural leader? Why or why not?

And lastly, how would others describe your desire to

• learn?

• improve?

• succeed?

• overcome obstacles?

• compete?

• work ethically?

• stand by your values?

- your integrity?

- share your personality?

- share your humor?

Here's a statement to practice:

- *Past employers would describe me as more than your average employee.*

If you haven't worked before, practice the statement below that fits you:

- *The people who know me best would describe me as more than your average college grad.*

- *The people who know me best would describe me as more than your average student.*

Now follow up the previous statement with this one: *The reason I say this is because* _____.

By making the opening statement, you reveal the qualities that make you special. Your follow-up statement provides the reason why. Now let's look at presenting yourself as an asset.

Exercise: Know Your Assets

Talk to your friends, family members, coworkers, former teachers, and former managers and ask them what they believe are your greatest strengths. More than likely, you will be amazed to find what these people see in you. They might be qualities you never realized you had. Ask those people to provide specific examples of why they would make these statements about you. The supporting statements they give will be extremely valuable as you prepare to discuss your qualities with prospective employers.

Continue asking yourself, "How would the people that know me best describe me?" Allow them to speak freely about your personality, sense of humor, work ethic, values, morals, and passions.

For the sake of demonstration, I will use myself as an example. Then, let's evaluate each attribute and develop each one for interviewing purposes. Don't laugh at mine, okay?

People have described me as funny, energetic, hardworking, reliable, having high standards, caring, honest, and very tactful . . . well, most of the time! If I didn't know better, I would think of those as great descriptions to mention in a job interview. Now I would like you to take a full minute to describe me out loud. Take your time.

My guess is that you have no idea what to say, other than the adjectives I provided above because you truly don't know me, right? So think of the interview this way: if I were to mention to an employer the same laundry list from above, the employer would still have no idea who I really was. In fact, the employer has most likely heard the same attributes repeatedly from other candidates.

English composition teachers usually tell their students, "Show, don't tell." The same valuable advice applies to job interviews.

Principle No. 2: Stories are more powerful than facts. (Facts tell, but stories sell.)

One of my goals for this book is to show you how to bring your character traits to life during an interview through anecdotes and examples. I use my traits not to boast, but to demonstrate an activity that will help you flesh out potential statements for the interview. Think of this as a brainstorming session. When you sit down to do this exercise for yourself, don't worry if you don't have much life experience. This activity is intended to help you grasp the concept. Write without judging yourself. You may not use all the content that comes out of this exercise, but you won't get the good stuff unless you get started. Here are mine.

Step 1: List your attributes.

Funny, energetic, hardworking, reliable, having high standards, caring, honest, and tactful.

Step 2: Tell me more.

Let's think about each adjective and expand on each one. Delve deeper into why people used these adjectives to describe you and write down whatever comes to mind.

- funny: good sense of humor, sarcastic

- energetic: high energy

- hard worker: puts in more than required

- reliable: consistent, can set your watch to him

- high standards: always striving to improve himself and people around him

- caring: good-hearted

- honest: trusted

- tactful: can give critical feedback without hurting someone's feelings

Step 3: Prove it.

Review your work in the previous phase. Imagine yourself as a fly on the wall of your own funeral. Your friends, family, and ex-coworkers are reminiscing about how compassionate, intelligent, and creative you were. They are sharing stories about you. Maybe this sounds silly, but the point is to get you thinking of concrete examples or incidents that bring your attributes to life. In other words, if "persistent" is a word that describes you, prove it with a story. For example, let's say you tested twenty-seven marketing strategies over two years before you were able to get a steady flow of clients. That's persistence! The proof is called your statement of credibility.

Here is how I would do this exercise if I were preparing for an interview:

Attribute: funny

Tell me more: good sense of humor, king of the one-liners, sarcastic, but very tactful

Prove it: Retained a long-standing relationship with a customer who was on the verge of leaving. He used his unique ability to bring a little levity to the conversation. Customer laughed, but he still has their business. Always has a smile on his face.

Attribute: hard worker

Tell me more: puts in more than required, has reputation for being the first to arrive and last to leave

Prove it: Prior employer used him for example to other recruiters to emulate due to his superb work ethic. Definitely not your average worker. Has an internal engine that never shuts down.

Attribute: reliable

Tell me more: consistent, never have to question whether he will be on time

Prove it: Worked for prior employer for nine years and had one sick day. Guy is like clockwork. If the doors are open, he will be there.

Attribute: has high standards

Tell me more: makes things better, always strives to improve himself and people around him

Prove it: His life is driven by self-imposed goals. He set out to earn an annual national award and reached his goal seven out of nine years.

Attribute: caring

Tell me more: good-hearted, gives of himself to others

Prove it: volunteer chaplain over twenty years

Attribute: honest

Tell me more: trusted, well-respected for his integrity

Prove it: Voted treasurer of his church for twenty years. You can give him your wallet and never worry.

Attribute: tactful

Tell me more: can give critical feedback without hurting someone's feelings

Prove it: He gives constructive criticism at nearly every one-on-one meeting with his team members. They typically comment on how the feedback energizes them rather than brings them down.

By starting with the initial comments and expanding on them, you can provide a snapshot of who you are and the value that you can bring. With information formulated from this exercise, you'll have plenty to say that will show the interviewer the real you.

Now let's see an example of how I would use this exercise to translate to the actual interview. Just to clarify ahead of time, I offer the example dialogue below in order to demonstrate. Even if you're not given the opportunity to answer such a general question, you may have the opportunity to touch upon all of your attributes at various points throughout the interview.

Interviewer: *What can you bring to the table?*

Interviewee: *Integrity is very important to me. Several people have noted the care and concern I have for others and described me as a person they could trust. I have been a volunteer chaplain for more than twenty years and my church's treasurer for twenty years. One member described me by saying that he felt that he could give me his wallet and wouldn't have been surprised to get it back with even more money than it originally had. I can assure you that you can put your faith and trust in me.*

Interviewer: *I like what I hear. Do you have any final comments?*

Interviewee: *To summarize, many have described me as having an engine that never shuts down because I am so driven to make a difference. I believe that I have the ability to make a difference wherever you choose to put me in your organization. Also, just so you don't get the wrong impression, even though I am driven, I love to have fun and make the workplace fun. I truly enjoy making people laugh. I believe that when employees are happy and smiling, good things happen. At my present company, I was able to turn a very difficult situation with a VIP client into a very positive experience by interjecting a bit of humor. Other coworkers have described me as positive, upbeat, and always having a smile on my face. With the characteristics I've mentioned, I would love to have the opportunity to positively influence your organization as well. Now that you have gotten a snapshot of me, what are your thoughts?*

Listen, listen, listen. (In a later chapter, I explain why this is so important.)

Do you see the difference? If I would have merely stated that I was funny, energetic, or trustworthy, I would have sounded like the dozens of other candidates trying to get the job. But because I weaved in specific examples that illustrated the characteristics I claimed to have, my responses were powerful. When you tell stories that back up your statements about yourself, the employer gets a close-up view of the real you.

Let me to provide another example of a fictional character named Amanda Trandle, who just graduated from college two months ago. She has very little work experience, but notice how she builds upon each attribute from her academic and volunteer experiences.

Attribute: caring

Tell me more: always concerned for others

Prove it: volunteer at hospice center helping families cope with the death of loved ones

Attribute: fearless

Tell me more: ignores advice from others whenever it sets limits

Prove it: In her first two years of college, she planned to major in design engineering and follow in her father's footsteps. Her father had strong connections in the design engineering industry and promised her a cushy job at his consulting firm as soon as she earned her engineering degree. However, after she had taken several engineering courses in her first two years, she realized she was not passionate about going into that field. So she experimented with non-engineering courses and internships and decided to minor in business during her junior year.

Attribute: driven

Tell me more: Barriers don't exist for her.

Prove it: Her business courses were challenging at first because she had no real world experience with which to understand the concepts. Still, she persisted because she knew she had the right instincts for business. One semester, she interned at a manufacturing company and impressed her managers because she applied the concepts from her business classes to her internship and vice versa.

So how would this exercise be incorporated in an interview setting?

Interviewer: *Tell me about yourself, Amanda.*

Interviewee: *Thank you for taking the time to meet with me. Most people who know me have told me that I have strong convictions and am extremely driven. When I come across a barrier, I figure out a way to get past it. In fact, this is why I studied design engineering in college in addition to having a minor in business. My father is a design engineer and he's had his own private consulting firm for many years now. I've always admired his love for engineering and had initially thought I was meant to pursue this as a career also. It was always my father's dream to see me earn my engineering degree and become a partner in his consulting firm. But during my junior year, I interned at a manufacturing company and realized that I was more driven toward business and people. I love the idea of managing in a fast-paced manufacturing environment. So I elected to go against my father's plan and focus on studying business. In addition to my schooling, I've been volunteering at a local hospice center for the last four years. It can be emotionally draining at* *times, but I feel fortunate to be able to help people during difficult times.*

Okay, now it's your turn. Download the worksheet entitled "Know Your Assets" from www.directionalmotivation.com and use it to list, expand on, and prove your attributes. This might be a tough exercise for some of you. Preparation for a successful interview is never easy, but it's definitely worth your time and effort. If you struggle, send me a message through www.directionalmotivation.com and I will be happy to assist you. If you have little to no experience at this point in your life, don't worry. Let's build from where you are.

CHAPTER 2
THE PURPOSE OF THE
JOB INTERVIEW

Those intimidated by job interviews tend to feel as though they are being examined under a microscope. I can understand that perspective. You're sitting across from a manager who has studied your resume and is observing how you answer every single question. Maybe that person is wondering why you never did a summer internship. Maybe he is wondering why it took you six years to graduate from college. Maybe that person is looking at your beat-up shoes, wondering what you were thinking when you put them on this morning.

The problem with that perspective is that you, the job applicant, are at the mercy of the employers. I'm here to tell you that you have complete control over what the microscope reveals. The person asking you questions wants to see beyond the surface. When the interviewer asks a question, he is hoping for the answer to reveal deeper qualities and characteristics about you. This is the real purpose of the interview.

Instead of a microscope, visualize a camera. You can't change the object being photographed, but you have the ability to monitor the lighting, adjust the lens, zoom in or out, or focus on an area that produces the best image. You are responsible for making the interviewer understand you. There are times when the lens will be pointed at an unattractive image. Still, the camera is in your hands and regardless of the types of questions coming at you, you are in control.

Your interviewing goal is to quickly and precisely convey the information an employer needs to know. The interview is not just an exchange of data. If employers simply wanted information about your skills and qualifications, they would save time and money by e-mailing you the questions and asking you to respond in writing. Or the decision might be based solely on how well you do on a test. Employers invite you for an interview because they want to observe you and engage in a conversation with you.

Have you ever watched Charlie Brown? I'm sure you're familiar with the scenes of him in class. The teacher might be saying something valuable, but her statements don't register in Charlie's mind. Charlie can only hear, "Womp, womp, womp." Unfortunately, this same scenario plays out in unfocused interviews. When you are sitting across from the interviewer, repeating the information in your resume by listing your education, past jobs, and mentioning that you are a hard worker, your interviewer is hearing, "Womp, womp, womp."

Your assets should be obvious when you tell your story during a job interview. The interviewer should not—and will not—pry it out of you!

Principle No. 3: Clarity is key. Make them understand. Don't make them guess.

You can approach an interview in two ways: reactive or proactive. Reactive is nothing more than responding to the specific question and simply providing an answer. Proactive is engaging in the conversation. When asked a question, provide the answer, but also give examples that will draw the interviewer's focus without being asked to elaborate. In that interview room, you are your own agent, publicist, advertising, and marketing department. Work hard for yourself. Take advantage of every opportunity to show what an amazing addition you would make to the company.

To illustrate my point, I offer the hypothetical example of Rhonda Taylor. Notice that by limiting her response to a few basic facts, she misses the opportunity to illustrate her uncanny maturity and business savvy.

Employer: *So Miss Taylor, I see that you attended Smythe University.*

Interviewee: *Yes, I did. My mom and dad thought it would be a good place for me to attend because it was so close to home. It allowed me to live off-campus even in my freshman year. Oh and tuition was cheaper.*

So what did the employer hear? Let's journey into the mind of the employer: *Nice enough person, but . . .*

- *Mom and Dad chose where she went to college. They probably coddled her all her life.*

- *She needed to be close to home. She is not mature and can't venture far from Mommy and Daddy.*

- *She lived off-campus starting from freshman year. She must not have wanted to socialize with her peers.*

- *Saving money on tuition was more important than finding a high-quality educational institution. She puts no real value on education.*

The employer has heard all that he wants to hear, interpreted the information, and the rest is "Womp, womp, womp." He is not impressed with Rhonda's story, and from this point forward, nothing she adds to the conversation is going to change his mind. The interview ends with the employer saying that he will get back to her in a couple of weeks with a final decision.

News flash! The decision not to hire her has already been made. Rhonda leaves the interview frustrated, realizing that she didn't connect with the employer.

It's a sad story, but it didn't need to be. Now let's hear Rhonda's real story:

After obtaining an SAT score of 1956 and being recognized for the groups she chaired including student body president, she received scholarship offers from several big, high-ranking universities. Her parents preferred that she attend one of those schools, but respected her decision to opt for a small liberal arts college. Rhonda's father had been disabled in a car accident during her senior year of high school, preventing him from managing the family car wash business. By selecting a university close to home, Rhonda was able to work weekends and contribute to the family income. She purchased a fourplex during her freshman year, which she lived in and managed during college. Upon graduation, she put the fourplex up for sale and planned to use the profit to pay off her school loans.

Wow! What a drastically different version from what the employer heard.

Stating facts about yourself never captures anyone's attention. Facts don't convey what's on the inside, and they certainly don't make you stand out from your competition. I hope that you truly understand the wise axiom, "Facts tell, but stories sell."

All too often, both the interviewer and the job applicant end up leaving the interview disappointed. Candidates answer the questions, but their real stories never see the light of day. In Rhonda's case, the employer was seeking a self-motivated, responsible individual whom he could train and mentor. He wasn't looking for particular skills. Instead, he was focused on finding certain character traits such as integrity, persistence, and courage. The employer knew that anyone with these traits could be trained and eventually develop into top performers at the company. Rhonda had all of those attributes, but she had no idea how to tell her story.

Now, imagine an alternative scenario in which Rhonda takes control of the interview. Here's what happened: She rehearsed her story in advance and in the process, became aware of how to tweak her story by rephrasing a few areas. For example, instead of saying she lived close to home, she said she lived close to her disabled father. Instead of saying she decided to live off-campus, she said she decided to manage a rental property. So in the revised happy ending, what did the employer hear? Let's journey into the mind of the employer again.

What she told me: *She had scholarships to attend top tier universities, but gave up those opportunities to help her family.*

What that means for the company: *She puts the needs of others before her own and is willing to sacrifice. She'll make a great team player.*

What she told me: *She worked nights and weekends while being a full-time student.*

What that means for the company: *She has a strong work ethic and understands the value of commitment.*

What she told me: *She figured out a way to live closer to home while building equity that would help her pay off student loans in the future.*

What that means for the company: *Smart girl. Coming out of high school, she was already thinking about how to get out of debt and make her living situation work for her. That's more than most teenagers would ever consider! She has foresight. She's conscientious, entrepreneurial, and has already learned the art of managing people and assets. She's not afraid of taking risks.*

I hope these theoretical examples drive home my point about the purpose of the job interview. Both you and the employer will benefit from having your story come out.

CHAPTER 3
PREPARATION: THE CRITICAL ACTIVITY FOR EVERY JOB INTERVIEW

By now, you should be able to see the root of the disconnect between the unsuccessful interviewee and the probing interviewer. As a recruiter, I've heard both sides every single day for the last twenty years. In fact, I'd be willing to bet that most job applicants get rejected from positions not because of lack of qualifications, but because of how they present themselves. So let's move on to how to prepare yourself to show the real you.

Do Your Research

This is common sense advice, but I cannot stress enough the importance of researching the company where you hope to land a job. Too many times, I have had job applicants skip this step, either through procrastination, lack of interest, or laziness. We live in the information era, where unlimited data is available at the click of a button. We look at menus before we set foot in a restaurant. We read movie reviews and ask our friends on Facebook or Twitter for input before buying movie tickets. We know the price of an item at five different retailers before we buy it. So why wouldn't we put the time into learning as much as we possibly can about a company before trying to land a job there?

Aren't you genuinely curious to learn more about a company where you could end up spending eight hours of your day, five days a week?

Most companies will provide information on the history, mission, staff size and more on their websites. Websites such as LinkedIn and Glassdoor offer valuable information such as company contacts, salaries, and how the company ranks against competitors. Use the Directional Motivation company worksheet available on our website www.directionalmotivation.com to list the information you find about each company where you are applying. These worksheets will be especially useful in getting organized if you are applying at multiple companies in the same industry.

Prepare to speak about what impresses you about the company, its culture, or style of management, or even better, how it compares to its competitors. As you uncover more information about the company, consider why you would like to be a part of the company and what you have to offer this one in particular.

In addition to finding information about the company, find out who will interview you. If you are working with a staffing or recruitment agency, your recruiter can typically provide this information, along with some background on each individual. Try to find your interviewer's history with the company and his or her educational and professional background. Even if your recruiter cannot offer that information, this should be easy to find on your own. LinkedIn is one of the best online resources for learning more about your professional contacts. However, don't limit yourself. Try a simple Google search in addition to LinkedIn. You might find that you attended the same university, worked for the same company, or even know the same people. You might discover, for example, that the interviewer's professional area of expertise is exactly what you studied in college. Whatever you find about the interviewer will help you make a connection, regardless of whether it relates to the open position.

As you read about the company and your interviewer, write down follow-up questions that demonstrate your thorough research and curiosity about the company.

Practice for the Perfect Interview

You've already heard the old adage, "Practice makes perfect." But less than perfect practice always produces less than perfect results. Find a volunteer interviewer who can be both supportive and critical (not of you, but of your answers). Practice explaining to your volunteer interviewer who you are and what makes you different. Practice talking about what you've learned about the company. Can you explain its track record and why you want to work there? These are very basic, but once you start to say these words out loud and become familiar with these statements as they leave your mouth, you will begin to feel more confident and more at ease.

I want you to engage in a slightly masochistic brainstorming session. Ask yourself why would you not hire you? No candidate is 100 percent perfect. What information from your resume might make an employer object to hiring you? Are you short on work experience? Did you work in a different field? Do you have additional classes to take before you can be certified or licensed? Are there photographs online of you dancing on a bar during spring break three years ago? (Okay, some of these things you should be able to figure out how to fix without reading this book. Take the scandalous pictures off of Facebook!) But take each possible objection and think of how you could address each one. You may not be able to overcome an employer's objections. But that's okay. As you continue to get feedback, you'll be prepared and know what you need to do to make yourself a serious candidate.

Face the Tough Questions

I'm sure you've heard that the best way to get over your fears is to face them. Remember the monster hiding in the closet? At some point, you made yourself open the closet door and only then were you able to get over that fear. When you decided to open the door, it was a proactive decision. Now, as you prepare for the job interview, you must face the dreaded difficult questions.

I've prepared tens of thousands of applicants for job interviews through two decades, and I've noticed that they tend to be most fearful of the questions that call them out on their faults. Surprisingly, many people walk into interviews prepared to talk about all their good qualities and life experiences, hoping the interviewer will not address, for example, a year gap in employment or quick turnover from one job to the next. The thought of being asked about a past failure and being forced to revisit a difficult time can be so excruciatingly dreadful for some that they avoid thinking about it altogether.

If you want to have a successful interview, you have no choice. You must face your past and prepare to explain yourself. How you explain yourself will reveal your character. Rather than taking a defensive stance and blaming others for setbacks, consider the tough question your opportunity to tell a story that will leave your interviewer feeling good about you. Through all my years of recruiting, I have found that honesty always wins out in the end. We're all human after all, and we all make mistakes!

When preparing how to answer these questions, recall Principle No. 3 from Chapter 2, "Clarity is key. Make them understand. Don't make them guess."

Think about the interviewer's point of view and what would make you sound like a whiny kid full of excuses versus a mature, likable professional. The key is to show the interviewer what you have learned from those experiences and how much smarter, wiser, more adaptable, and more resilient you have become since then.

Here are five of the most common objections in the job interview:

1) "Why did you leave your last job?"

I've heard some applicants start to answer this question by saying right off the bat, "Well, I was fired." In this case, that immediately throws up red flags for the interviewer. It's difficult to win someone over after such a blunt statement.

First, make sure you are using the correct terms. If you were laid off, this is not the same thing as being fired. Layoffs are quite common, so feel free to briefly explain the company's economic hardships that led to the layoffs. Some details are worth including. If you managed to stay onboard at your previous company through three different layoffs, for example, that's important. If you were the last person standing in your department, include that detail. It shows that your employer held onto you for as long as possible.

If you were terminated, tread very carefully here. Ease into it. The artful interviewee can engage the interviewer from the beginning of the story and walk that person through the details leading up to the termination. Start with something positive and then transition into the termination. If done right, the interviewer will wholeheartedly relate to you by the end of the story. Here's an example:

Initially, they promoted me to supervisor because they noticed how well-respected I was among my coworkers. In fact, my boss told me that upper management intended to transition from a traditional style of management to a more team-based culture. They had hoped I could help motivate the junior team members to improve customer service and increase sales in our branch. In the first three months, I led my team up to No. 1 from among the lowest producing branches in our region. But soon after, I realized that—despite upper management's directive to move toward a team-based culture—the company's operations weren't quite ready for my self-empowering management style. When it became clear our management styles were too different, they decided to let me go. I have listed several references that would be happy to vouch for the way I manage teams. Does your organization embrace a more engaging style of management?

Notice how much easier it is to relate to this person when the details are framed just right. In the example above, the interviewee takes the spotlight off of being fired and succeeds in showing more valuable attributes. Before explaining that you were terminated, try to show why the previous company hired you and what you accomplished while you were there.

Stories about mismanagement are common, but don't go on and on about your previous company's horrible management style and how poorly you were treated. If you were truly at fault, be honest. Tell the story about how your firing served as a wake-up call for you to communicate more clearly, to learn how to relate to your coworkers more effectively, or to search for a company that shared your values.

Differentiate the "real you" from the termination. For example:

To be honest with you, I feel so bad about what happened. In hindsight, I believe the repetitive nature of the job led me to go on autopilot. I didn't perform to the level that I should have, but I've learned so much since then.

Great managers have most likely experienced personal setbacks early in their careers. If you tell your story well, they may identify with your situation and might even become an advocate for you.

I want to reinforce my point that we're all human and we all make mistakes. Bosses make huge mistakes when they fail to recognize that their employees' so-called "mistakes" could actually be manifestations of genius. As a fun side note, I discovered an article on the website of *Business Insider* that lists seventeen people who were fired before they became rich and famous. Here are several of my favorite examples:

- Walt Disney's newspaper editor told the aspiring cartoonist he wasn't creative enough. (I think he had a bit of a creative genius.)

- J.K. Rowling was fired for spending too much time brainstorming story ideas at work. (It would appear that her brainstorming paid off.)

- A Baltimore TV producer told Oprah that she was "unfit for television news." (Yeah, I guess they were right . . . TV would never work for her.)

- Sitcom producers didn't like the way Jerry Seinfeld was playing a part and cut him out of the script. (So why play a part when you can just be . . .YOU?)

- The manager of the Grand Ole Opry told Elvis that he was better off driving trucks. (I think a few record producers are glad he didn't take that advice to heart.)

- Mark Cuban lost his job as a salesman at a computer store. (I think he figured out what this "computer thing" was all about.)

- Bill Belichick was fired from his first head coaching job for an unsuccessful season. (Three Super Bowl victories later, maybe management realized they reacted too hastily.)

So you see, getting fired doesn't have to be a topic of conversation that makes you cringe. Think of it as a necessary part of your journey to greatness.

2) "Your resume shows a year-long gap in employment."

The job market is rough, so it's no surprise to employers to see gaps in employment. Still, they want to know how you spent that time and what steps you took to find another job. Free time is a luxury most people don't have, and if your interviewer gets the sense that you spent your time off napping on the couch, milking your unemployment benefits, you'll suddenly become very unappealing. Demonstrate that you took advantage of that time to improve your skills, explore interests in other industries, do pro bono work, or launch an entrepreneurial venture. Even if all you did was manage to keep yourself motivated and optimistic despite the tough job market, that's worth mentioning.

If you are grimacing because you didn't do any of these things during your time off, start now! Search for a webinar, podcast, or book about your trade or any kind of self-improvement. Delve into that source even if the interview is only two days away. When the interviewer asks you what you did while unemployed, you could mention that resource and explain how it has helped you improve yourself. Many times, merely demonstrating personal initiative can land you a position over your competition. Stay active and keep growing!

If you had a personal circumstance that prevented you from working, such as caring for a sick family member or a newborn baby, explain that. Talk about your accomplishments at your previous job and why you enjoyed your work there. From that point, you can transition to discussing your current situation and explaining how circumstances have changed. Your interviewer is a regular person just like everybody else and is fully capable of relating to personal issues such as family obligations.

3) "You haven't had much experience in this field. How are you qualified for this position?"

Everybody has to start somewhere. If you are applying for a job that you have never done professionally, think about the position and its responsibilities. Now think about your personal attributes and how well you have carried out those tasks in other areas of your life. Make a connection wherever possible.

For example, let's say you're interviewing for a job as a legal assistant and the job requires you to organize case files and draft documents. You've never worked at a law firm before, but you've worked at your university coordinating class schedules for the school of public health. Okay, so the two jobs appear totally unrelated at first glance. But in your previous campus job, you had a ton of student records to organize and professors' schedules to manage. You also drafted policy memos that were distributed to high-level administrators. When you interview for the legal assistant position, use those details as evidence of your skills in organization and written communication. These skills are easily transferrable to another industry.

Interviewers will appreciate your honesty, so there is no need to exaggerate your experience or worse, lie to appear qualified. The important point to get across is your drive and initiative.

Here is another example of how you can artfully answer this tough question:

There was a similar concern with my previous job when I first started there because I didn't have the experience for that role. But my managers soon realized that they had made the right decision because of my quick study approach and my determination. To be honest with you, I have not been trained in that area. But in many of my previous jobs, my managers have commented on how quickly I learn. I'm like a sponge for knowledge. I just love to learn. Although I don't have this particular skill set, I can assure you that I'm committed to coming up to speed within the first two to three weeks.

Principle No. 4: Personality and professionalism outweigh skills.

Lack of skill seems to be the most common weakness that job applicants confide in me when I prepare them for interviews. I'm often surprised at how people underestimate themselves and their abilities. For some reason, many people believe that because they have not held a particular position in a particular industry for a particular amount of time, employers will not consider them to be qualified. This may be true for highly technical positions requiring graduate degrees. But in every job, you learn by doing. And if you believe in yourself enough to believe that you will learn the skills and excel at your job, your interviewers will see that. Give employers more credit by giving them the full picture. They deserve to learn more about your talents and past successes in order to determine whether you'll be able to contribute those to their company.

4) "Why can't you hold a job longer than six months?"

Often, candidates don't spell out on their resumes whether a job was an internship, contract position, part-time or full-time position. If you've had a string of contract jobs that ended after you completed a project, make sure to explain that. Don't make any assumptions that the interviewer will understand your circumstances. Did you accomplish a project faster than anticipated and move on to the next job? Did you learn new skills that prepared you for the next project at the other company? That's wonderful! Explain that.

If you are one of those habitual quitters because you simply weren't happy at a job, be careful of how you explain this. I've heard some candidates say they weren't being challenged, so they quit. Always try to avoid sounding negative during a job interview. Instead of focusing on why you left, focus on the opportunity you found at the next job. Highlight that your decision to move from one job to another was based on your desire to grow. Explain that your decisions worked out well for you because of what you learned and how quickly you picked up these new skills. Emphasize how you continued to develop yourself at each new job.

There is nothing wrong with moving on to new positions, as long as you're able to get the interviewer to understand your perspective and illustrate that you put considerable thought into your decisions. Employers don't want flaky, fickle employees who make spur-of-the-moment decisions.

If you're still ashamed of quitting multiple times, here is an excerpt from a Freakonomics Radio podcast hosted by Stephen Dubner titled "The Upside of Quitting" to put it all into perspective:

To help us understand quitting, we look at a couple of key economic concepts in this episode: sunk cost and opportunity cost. Sunk cost is about the past – it's the time or money or sweat equity you've put into a job or relationship or a project, and which makes quitting hard. Opportunity cost is about the future. It means that for every hour or dollar you spend on one thing, you're giving up the opportunity to spend that hour or dollar on something else – something that might make your life better. If only you weren't so worried about the sunk cost. If only you could .... quit.

5) "Your GPA is not quite as high as we'd like."

I work with many Fortune 500 companies that have a minimum grade point average required of anyone eligible for a position. HR managers have told me GPA is an important factor because they don't want to hire someone who is irresponsible or simply not bright. When companies are adamant about a minimum GPA, yes, it may be a challenge to get those companies to make an exception. Still, no situation is hopeless. I've made this point before and I'll remind you again: your interviewer is a regular person with feelings and life experiences and is capable of empathy. Your GPA is only a number. It may give a certain impression of you but don't let it determine your future. Use this as an opportunity to tell your story. If an employer has a set GPA minimum without exception, don't hang your head low. Keep moving forward. Not all companies have a minimum GPA and there is a company out there that needs you.

Here's an example of one story that shows how the interviewee manages to address this issue honestly while demonstrating his determination and renewed commitment to education:

Have you ever gotten yourself in a situation that you wished you could change? Let me explain it the best way I know how. I was really stupid when I first started college. High school had never been a challenge for me, so I took twenty-one credits during my first semester of college while holding a job waiting tables at night. I underestimated how much studying my classes would require and how significantly my part-time job would affect my energy level and sleeping habits. I ended up performing poorly in several classes my first year. After that, I cut down my work hours and course load and spent the next three years focused on my classes and bringing my GPA up. Although I did very well in my last two years, my low grades early on still affected my GPA. I've learned a lot about managing my time since then.

Behavior-based Interviewing

Now that you've done the most difficult part of your preparation, I'd like to introduce you to a specific style of interview questions. Behavior-based interviewing takes real-life situations that you may encounter in the workplace and asks you to provide examples of how you have handled these types of situations in prior settings. Many employers rely heavily on these questions because the answers speak volumes about the job applicant. Interviewers hope to understand your decision-making ability and thought processes in order to predict how you will respond to certain life and workplace scenarios.

Let's go through some of these questions and what information employers are seeking. I do not provide you specific responses because they must relate to your unique background. However, I do offer insights on what information the interviewer is looking for.

Here are some common behavior-based interview questions:

1) Tell me about a time when you worked for a difficult supervisor or managed a problematic subordinate. How did you resolve this situation?

What they really want to know: Is this the type of individual that will end up in the fetal position in a difficult environment, or will he find a way to overcome this situation? Will he blame someone else or take responsibility?

2) Tell me about a situation in which you failed. What did you learn from this experience and how have you applied this lesson in your life?

What they really want to know: Does this person persevere, regardless of hurdles? Does she take the pitfalls of life and use them to prepare herself for challenging situations in the future? Does she view these circumstances as developmental steps or does she complain that life wasn't fair?

3) Tell me about a time when you proposed an idea to your manager, but your manager did not use it. How did you respond to your manager? How did you communicate this development to subordinates and coworkers?

What they really want to know: Will this person become bitter when coworkers do not accept or act upon his ideas? Will he convey a negative spirit or attitude to peers and subordinates that will impact morale, or does he keep his spirits high and continue contributing to the team?

4) Tell us about a time in which you were asked to influence a group of people under your direction to take a certain course of action. What approach did you use and what was the outcome?

What they really want to know: Is this person a leader? Do others trust her, and will people follow her? Can she be put in positions of authority? Are her efforts successful?

5) If you were to start your life over, what changes or adjustments would you make? Why?

What they really want to know: Is this person willing to admit possible mistakes? What has he learned from his experiences? How has he applied this knowledge? How perceptive is he to changing trends?

6) Please provide us with a couple of examples in which you made a positive impact in your workplace environment. How would you accomplish this within our organization?

What they really want to know: Does this person have personal initiative to make a difference? Is she comfortable with the status quo or does she try to make things better?

7) How do you define leadership? What parts of your definition have you implemented in your own life? What have been the results?

What they really want to know: Does this person believe in building a team environment or is he more of an authoritarian? Is his answer fluff or can he back it up with clear examples?

8) If you were the CEO of a company and a person like yourself applied, would you hire that person? Why?

What they really want to know: What opinion does this person have of herself? What characteristics about herself does she value? These will be the same characteristics that she displays in our workplace.

9) What kinds of resources do you use to improve your skills?

What they really want to know: Does this person strive to improve himself? Is he open to change? What principles does this person value and how does he apply them in his professional life?

10) How would you describe your most difficult boss? What changes would you suggest to that boss? What have you learned from the experience of working for this person?

What they really want to know: By describing her most difficult boss, she will demonstrate the issues that she really struggles with.

It will also reveal if the source of the problem was the boss or the employee. Will the person value the negative experience and change her own management style to avoid making the same mistakes, or will she stick to venting about her old boss?

Unfortunately, I've heard from too many employers that job applicants go to the interview without ever having thought about any of these scenarios. When these behavior-based questions come up, many interviewees have responded with, "I don't think I can answer that," or "Wow, I guess I never have thought about this."

These are several examples of behavior-based questions. Use them as a rough guide to help you think of specific examples that would demonstrate your abilities in each of these areas. I also encourage you to go to www.directionalmotivation.com for more examples. If you are having trouble crafting answers, send me a message through www.directionalmotivation.com and I would be happy to assist you.

Don't Forget to Plan Logistics

Lastly, your preparation should include planning your schedule, how to get to the interview, and mastering the science of arrival.

Clear your schedule for the entire day if you are having an on-site interview. If the interviewer perceives that you'll benefit the company, that person may give you a tour and have you meet with other managers. These are good signs! By giving yourself flexibility, you will be in a position to accommodate such requests.

Know the physical location of your interview. I suggest not only mapping your route a couple of days beforehand and checking traffic patterns, but also driving to your destination to do a test run. If you rely solely on getting directions from online maps, you might encounter unexpected one-way streets or blocked off construction zones. If you run into an unforeseen problem on the way to the interview, call the employer. Keep the conversation short. Long-winded sob stories are annoying. When you arrive—albeit later than scheduled—be sure to let the interviewer know the effort you put into trying to show up on time. Even if your logistics haven't worked out at this point, at least it gives you the opportunity to demonstrate that you thought ahead.

Be prompt. Arrive no sooner than fifteen minutes early, but no later than five minutes early. If you arrive prior to fifteen minutes you may end up sitting for an extended period of time, creating a potentially awkward situation with the receptionist. You also don't want to look desperate.

CHAPTER 4
YOUR MESSAGE WITHOUT SAYING A WORD

In speaking with hiring managers, human resource representatives, and other recruiters, I have discovered that the decision to hire typically crystallizes in the first two to five minutes of an interview. So the sooner you communicate your strengths to a prospective employer, the better. As you already know, communication is far beyond the spoken and written word. It's not only what you say, but how you say it. The image you portray through your body movements, gestures, eye contact, posture, and, of course, actions plays a huge role in the first impression you give to your interviewer.

As an executive recruiter, I have been the recipient of some very embarrassing feedback from companies who have interviewed candidates arranged by my agency. These calls will typically begin with a question such as, "Have you ever seen this candidate?" or "Did you have the opportunity to discuss our company dress code with this individual?" In these cases, the impression the candidates left had nothing to do with the words that came out of their mouths.

I'm sure you've heard all the basics of effective nonverbal communication during a job interview: show a winning smile, look the interviewer in the eye, give a firm handshake, sit up straight, dress the part, etc. These are all good advice, but the last thing I want to do is give you a long list of bodily gestures to do or not do. Nonverbal cues should come naturally if you have the right intentions behind them. So I'm keeping my advice simple: Your nonverbal messages should display your energy, authenticity, and professionalism. If they do, you're good.

Pre-Interview Exercise

Social psychologist Amy Cuddy gave a fascinating TED talk about body language. She studies power dynamics, specifically nonverbal expressions of power and dominance. (I highly recommend all job seekers to watch her twenty-minute video online. You may access the link from www.directionalmotivation.com and the References section at the end of this book.) In the video, Cuddy explains that throughout the animal kingdom, we all express feelings of power through body language by making ourselves bigger. When we feel powerless, we tend to hunch down and make ourselves smaller. Unfortunately, people tend to spend the final moments before an interview sitting down in a slouched position. Body language is very important. No slouching in the lobby or in the interview room!

Here is the exercise that she recommends to everybody during the final moments before a job interview: Go to the bathroom or some private area and spend two minutes with your chin slightly lifted and arms outstretched in a V-shape, upwards and outwards. This is called a power pose, and holding this pose will significantly impact your presence during the interview. Do this before any situation in which you will be evaluated. Since the exercise is done in private, it's not meant to illustrate your power to the interviewer. Instead, it's about using your body to feel powerful from within, which will inherently show "the real you" to the interviewer.

As Cuddy explains, "Our bodies change our minds and our minds change our behavior and our behavior changes our outcomes." Pretty cool how it works!

Practice Your Unspoken Messages

The best way to evaluate your nonverbal communication skills and work on improving them is to practice in a way that allows you to physically look at yourself. You could practice in the mirror, but that can easily get distracting. If you practice solely in front of the mirror, you might spot a zit or a piece of food in your teeth. Random thoughts like, "Oh wow! I look exhausted," might perplex you. At that point, all concentration goes out the window. So for the bulk of your nonverbal communication practice, I recommend video recording yourself practicing every step of the interview: your greeting, guiding the interviewer through your resume, telling stories or giving examples that back up descriptions of yourself, asking questions about the company, and making your final statements. If you have a friend who can volunteer to be your practice interviewer, that's wonderful. If not, you can easily do it alone.

I know I don't need to hold your hand through the logistics of video recording yourself. Fortunately, technology makes it possible to do this for free. Use your smartphone, your computer program, or Skype.

As you practice, consider the following principle (I saved the best for last!):

Principle No. 5: The interviewer is the most important person on the face of the planet.

Keeping this principle in mind will definitely impact how well you present yourself as you practice.

Keep Your Energy Up

Have you ever gone to the DMV or the post office on a busy day and noticed how the staffers go through the motions like zombies? I've noticed many times that the customer service agents are so swamped and tired of dealing with problem customers that they appear to have no energy. Their voices are monotone, they look straight at their computer monitors, and they generally appear to have no interest in you. The other person's energy makes a huge difference for me as a customer. Whenever I'm dealing with a horrible customer service agent either in person or over the phone, my gut reaction is to end the experience as quickly as possible.

Now put yourself in the position of the interviewer, who is also a customer. How would you feel if the person sitting across from you is sitting slouched in the chair, appearing bored? What if that person is gazing out the window, appearing aloof, as she twirls her hair with her finger or taps her pen against her armrest? First of all, you'd most likely find it offensive that the interviewee is wasting your time because that person does not seem interested in the company. When you stop and think about whether this person is someone you'd want to hire, what characteristics do these gestures reflect? They illustrate laziness, lack of ambition, maybe even a lack of concern for one's surroundings.

Granted, many of us—including me—have nervous habits we do unconsciously. Watching yourself beforehand can make you aware of those habits and consciously replace them with other nonverbal cues that are much more desirable.

Smiling is, without a doubt, the best nonverbal gesture you can do in a job interview to keep your energy high and show interest. Even if you're not in the mood to smile at first, do it. I promise it will end up being a genuine smile in less than thirty seconds. You'll be amazed at the effectiveness of a smile in making a connection with another person in any situation. So smile as if your bank account depended on it—because it does.

Authenticity

You may be able to say all the right words, but if your actions or outward appearance do not reflect your statements, there is nothing you can say that will convince an employer to hire you. Act the part from the moment you begin corresponding with the employer through phone calls and e-mails all the way through the end of the interview.

For example, let's say you describe yourself as organized and efficient. See the following situations and tell me which one backs up your statement:

>a) You rush into the office two minutes late, holding an overstuffed bag with loose papers and battery chargers.

>b) You walk in ten minutes early holding a leather case with a legal pad, extra copies of resumes, and any paperwork prepared ahead of time.

Or let's say you describe yourself as curious and inquisitive. Tell me which one backs up your statement:

>a) When the employer asks if you have any questions, you wait a half second and respond, "No, I don't. Thank you."

>b) You ask questions throughout the interview based on your earlier research of the company.

These character traits are especially important if they are critical aspects of the position. So let's say you are applying for a customer service position and you claim to be cheerful, friendly, and easygoing. See which scenario would help or hinder you:

a) You walk in with your head hung low, pass by the receptionist without even a nod, and then complain to the interviewer's assistant that he gave you faulty directions.

b) You walk in with a bright smile and greet the first person you see.

The right thing to do is obvious in each of these situations, but when you have the pre-interview jitters, common sense sometimes goes out the door. Always remain conscious of your nonverbal cues.

The Technician Who Left Them Speechless

One of the most poignant stories I've heard that clearly illustrates how actions speak louder than words came from an HR manager at a biotech company. Her company was developing a nano medical device and hiring microassembly technicians to build prototypes. Microassembly technicians must be highly dexterous with their hands because they manufacture devices using tiny parts under a microscope. Because this particular position was building medical devices in a cleanroom laboratory where environmental pollutants are kept to a bare minimum, these technicians were required to follow strict cleanliness rules.

Imagine the interviewer's reaction when one applicant showed up, reeking of cigarette smoke and his hands shaking uncontrollably. It didn't matter what he said during the interview or how well he said it. He didn't have to say a word.

Professionalism

I have spoken and written about professionalism extensively throughout my career. I could probably write volumes about what professionalism means because I am truly passionate about career development. In fact, all of the advice I offer in this book is meant to help you showcase your professionalism. However, as it relates to nonverbal communication during interviews, employers simply want to observe how you conduct yourself at work. That includes everything from how you dress and react to how you speak. I'd like to start with a few obvious examples and funnel it down to the more subtle ways you can demonstrate your professionalism.

The Notorious Flip Flops

One of the more embarrassing conversations I've had with a client was with a manager from a well-known food manufacturer. This is a Fortune 500 company that literally receives hundreds of resumes every day. In preparing the candidate for his interview for a production supervisor position, I mentioned that business casual would be the appropriate attire given the company's relaxed culture. Of course, by business casual, I meant slacks and a freshly ironed button-down or polo shirt. The candidate—we'll call him Jay—had a different understanding of business casual. I later heard from the HR manager we can call Damien, who mentioned that the interviewers were very impressed with Jay's communication skills and leadership qualities. In fact, when a candidate has done well

on a phone interview, the management team invites the candidate for an in-person interview at an exclusive country club. This was also the case with Jay. He had performed exceptionally well on his phone interview, and the executives were excited to meet him at the country club. However, Damien explained that he was extremely embarrassed to conduct an interview, attended by the company's top-level executives, of a young man dressed in cargo shorts and flip flops. As much as the team felt Jay's qualifications made him a good fit for the company, they couldn't overlook his lack of common sense in wearing vacation attire to a job interview. Jay had blown it big time.

When I reported back to Jay, I thought he was going to cry. He said when he heard the word "casual," he never gave it a second thought. I am sure that Jay is still haunted by the thought of how close he came to joining such a sought-after company.

Please don't make the same mistake. You can always dress down after you arrive, but you can never dress up. If you show up to a job interview dressed inappropriately, you will have a very uncomfortable experience. Worse, you may miss the opportunity of a lifetime.

"Just a sec, I need to take this."

I hesitated about whether to tell my readers never to answer their cell phones during a job interview. Should I tell you never to whip out a skewered corn on the cob during an interview and start eating it? Of course not! It's glaringly obvious. Isn't it difficult to fathom how anyone could do that? Unfortunately, I have heard of many instances of job applicants sabotaging themselves by picking up their cell phones during interviews, so I decided I had to address this problem. I understand the compulsion to reach for your cell phone. Much has been written about the cell phone being "the new cigarette." In 2008, British researchers coined a new term "nomophobia"—short for "no-mobile-phone phobia"— to describe the fear of being without a cell phone. At this point, I remind you of Principle No. 5: The interviewer is the most important person on the face of the planet. Who is more important: your buddy on the line or the person who impacts your livelihood?

If you suffer from nomophobia, the solution is simple: Turn off your cell phone beforehand or better yet, leave it in the car. Don't set it on vibrate and think you'll be safe because let's face it, that setting can be as loud as a fat cat purring. Even if you do not give in to your instinct to answer the call or read the text message, you will get distracted and lose focus.

Subtle Nonverbal Signals Can Make All the Difference

Skilled interviewers catch the tiniest of details, including the manner in which the applicant makes a statement. To echo my previous points, this is one of the reasons you must be authentic and watch yourself very closely during practice sessions. Employers will be able to detect when you're merely putting on a show.

Listen intently to the interviewer's questions. Before responding, it's okay to pause for a moment to gather your thoughts. Silent pauses to reflect prior to responding can actually work well. Politicians, like former President Bill Clinton, tend to use this strategy. Rather than answering immediately, they may tilt their heads and hold a pensive facial expression. People appreciate it when you pause to concentrate because it shows that you are taking their questions very seriously.

The tiniest details make a big difference. Take your time in answering questions. Your answer is worth waiting for.

CHAPTER 5
THE BEGINNING OF THE INTERVIEW

I'm sure many of you have seen reality TV shows like *The X Factor* or *American Idol*. The scene is all too familiar:

"Go ahead, let's hear what you've got," a judge might say. The singer starts to belt out a tune, fully knowing the next moment could change her life forever. Two lines into the song, we hear Simon say, "Enough, please . . . no more. You're not the level of talent we are looking for." The contestant might plead, "No, wait, I can do better. I just need a second to compose myself." But the request is to no avail. The audition is over.

Show biz can be brutal, right? Job interviews don't happen in the exact same way. Thankfully, interviewers are typically not as harsh as Simon Cowell, formerly the host of *American Idol* and now, *The X Factor*. But they are quite similar. In the audition, the singer has less than thirty seconds to pique the judges' interest. That tiny window of time could either launch a new career or do nothing for it. Consider the job interview in the same light. If you don't capture the employer's interest immediately, that's it. The interviewer will be thinking, "Please, no more."

We discussed the importance of nonverbal communication in the previous chapter. The beginning of the interview is the most important time to focus on nonverbal strategies because, as we've learned from those reality TV contests, first impressions are lasting impressions, as the old saying goes. Send the right signals by smiling, keeping your eye contact firm, and all the other tips I mentioned in the previous chapter. I stress these points again here because at the beginning of the interview, it's easy to let your mind wander and become cluttered with worries:

This guy looks nice. Hopefully, he'll go easy on me.

I can't believe I almost missed my freeway exit!

Did I bring extra copies of my resume?

What time is it?

I knew it. I should have worn the other suit. It's cold in here!

Don't forget the story about how I set up and implemented the new system for the office and oh, of course, that award for my innovative tech idea!

Calm down. Make a conscious effort to stay clear and focused on your interviewer. You must listen to everything your interviewer is telling you. The connection you establish with your interviewer from the beginning will carry you through the end of the interview. And again, I'll remind you of Principle No. 5: The interviewer is the most important person on the face of the planet.

If your interviewer makes small talk, go with it. It's a good sign because it means she wants you to feel comfortable. This is the perfect time to establish rapport. Feel free to mention how unexpectedly pleasant the scenery was on your drive to the office or how beautiful the weather has been lately. Keep it positive! This is not the time to complain about the horrible traffic or your toothache.

If your interviewer appears stiff, grumpy, or inexperienced at interviewing, use your charming personality to warm up that person. Make it your goal to establish a genuine connection with the interviewer. Remember to smile, even if it isn't reciprocated at first. Throw out a few quick icebreaker questions or comments of your own. If you did your research, which is covered in Chapter 3, you might have discovered from the interviewer's LinkedIn profile that you once lived in the same city or commented on the same newspaper article that morning. This is the perfect opportunity to mention those tidbits! If you're struggling with finding something to say, keep it light. Mention how you appreciate the design of the office or the friendly receptionist at the front desk. If the interviewer gave you driving directions to the office, compliment that person on the clarity of the directions. If you can break down that wall and make the interviewer feel comfortable with you early on, it will make a huge difference for both of you throughout the entire process.

Many years ago, I took a Dale Carnegie class on communication. In this class, the instructor stressed how easy it is to make small talk using the acronym FORM, which stands for family, occupation, recreation, and message. Who doesn't like to talk about their family, work, or hobbies? There is no need to dread small talk conversations when there is so much to talk about if you consider this acronym. Practice it in everyday situations and you will be pleasantly surprised at how easy it will come to you.

Typically, job interviews start with the interviewer explaining the details of the position. It's absolutely crucial that you absorb the information from the beginning and make mental notes of the questions you will ask later. In fact, feel free to bring a notebook and pen so that you can take notes to formulate your questions later.

Use the first few moments to listen and observe your surroundings. Does this place appear to have a relaxed culture or is it more formal? Based on what you find, be flexible and tailor your approach and body language to send the right signals in either environment.

The Cast of Undesirable Characters

Sometimes, despite preparation, applicants fall into presenting themselves as the same ugly characters employers see time and again. Don't be one of these characters!

Bobby Bragger

When interviewing, Bobby Bragger starts most of his sentences describing how wonderful he is. Yes, we must demonstrate our talents and our abilities, but Bobby takes it to a whole new level by presenting himself alone as the answer to every problem. He never acknowledges the people around him or the people that have supported him. In job interviews, Bobby typically will not listen to the questions and cuts off the employers while they are talking, so that he can squeeze in more information about himself. He often indicates that the previous companies he worked for could not have survived without him. He concludes interviews in his classic narcissistic form: he lists what he expects to get from the employers before he could even consider an offer.

Why this doesn't work: Confidence is great, but not when it goes overboard to cockiness. When you dominate the interview in the Bobby Bragger fashion, you show that you lack integrity, listening skills, and basic manners. Additionally, most companies are looking for team players or at least individuals that can function well in a team environment. It's obvious that Bobby would be difficult to work with.

The cure for the bragger: If you have Bobby Bragger tendencies, take an honest assessment of yourself before going to another job interview. Sometimes, the bragger comes out when you're nervous or worried about your weaknesses. I encourage you to be genuine and honest about your skills and talents, as well as your weaknesses. Employers want people with integrity, particularly those who are able to recognize what they need to improve about themselves.

Marty Motormouth

You might initially think that Marty is pretty much like Bobby Bragger because he talks so much. The difference here is that many times, nerves seem to lubricate the jawbones and words end up spilling out. Marty typically is a caring, thoughtful type of person, but in his strong

yearning for acceptance, he tries to talk people into liking him. During job interviews, he rambles. Marty tells long-winded stories and goes off on tangents, leaving both people wondering how the conversation drifted so far from the original topic. Whenever that happens, Marty will typically chuckle and then apologize. And then he will do the same thing when responding to the next question! In the sales world, Marty is the one everyone likes, but often, he will talk beyond the close and lose the sale. In hindsight, he'll often think to himself, "Man, I never should have said that. They were ready to buy!" It happens the same way with his interviews. The company likes his skills and personality and thinks he could be a good hire. All of a sudden, out slips an off-the-wall comment and then poof! He kills his chances of getting hired.

Why this doesn't work: Employers don't want to deal with someone without an internal filter. Marty doesn't appear to be in control of what comes out of his mouth, and with that lack of control comes risk: He might offend a very important client. He might gab with his cubicle buddies and slow down everybody's productivity. He might divulge confidential information to the wrong person. No employer will want to hire someone who can potentially cause so many problems.

The cure for the motormouth: If you tend to talk nonstop, I urge you to slow down, listen, and respond with targeted responses. If you need a minute to think about your answer, go ahead and pause briefly. Silence is a thousand times better than rambling. Remember Principle No. 5: The interviewer is the most important person on the face of the planet. That means that person's time is valuable. Don't waste it!

Shirley Shyness

After coaching so many applicants like Shirley Shyness, I've learned that she isn't aware of her assets. She is scared of job interviews because she doesn't believe in herself. She typically answers questions with short "yes" or "no" responses and then looks to the ground while waiting for the next question. Interviewers struggle and sometimes, they even try to help Shirley by asking her easy opening questions to loosen her up. Unfortunately, Shirley is not comfortable talking about herself.

Why this doesn't work: If Shirley doesn't believe in herself, how can anyone else believe in her? Employers don't want someone who is unsure of her abilities or needs handholding. An applicant's lack of confidence to speak up can be interpreted in so many negative ways: *This person doesn't have the skills. She's socially awkward and* *doesn't have a clue about how to communicate. What happens when I assign this person a task outside of her comfort zone? How could she possibly manage people if she can't even look me in the eye?*

The cure for the shy: Preparation is the key. If you suffer from shyness, you need to determine what you can offer an employer and rehearse to yourself over and over until you believe them yourself. Review the exercises in chapters 1-4 of this book, particularly the exercise on knowing your assets in Chapter 1 and the power pose in Chapter 4. In fact, go ahead and do the power pose before your mock interviews. I mention in Chapter 4 that you could practice alone by recording yourself, but for you shy folks, I highly recommend practicing with someone you feel comfortable with. We all need cheerleaders in our lives, so go find yours. Let your cheerleaders tell you why they believe in you. If they believe in you, shouldn't you? During the interview, think of the interviewer as your cheerleader and let the real you come out. Remember my tip about smiling in Chapter 4. You will be amazed at what this will do for you!

CHAPTER 6
THE MIDDLE OF THE INTERVIEW

By now, you have captured the attention of your interviewer. Next comes the meaty part. This is the time for you to stretch your sensory abilities. In the middle of the interview, you must be doing several things simultaneously:

- listening and understanding the questions

- thinking of the best way to respond

- remembering the content you fleshed out from the exercises in the previous chapters of the book

- speaking clearly and intelligently

- keeping your energy high

- smiling

- sitting up straight

- maintaining eye contact

Yes, it sounds like a feat only a superhero can do. But you are capable of more than you know. Follow the example of one of my favorite animals: the duck. When we see them in a lake, they appear to be floating on the water magically. They're not flailing around, trying to stay above the water. Yet, we don't see the duck's little webbed feet paddling underneath the water at a hundred miles an hour. During an interview, your heart may be racing, but it is still possible to display confidence and professionalism. When you focus on your responses and engage the interviewer with your stories, you'll begin to feel more comfortable. I guarantee it.

ASK QUESTIONS

Employers will usually give the applicant an opportunity to ask questions about the position or the company. This is another chance for you to show your sincere enthusiasm for the position and what a breath of fresh air you would be for the company. Ask questions about the expectations of the position, the history and culture of the company, and the background of the interviewer.

Here are some examples:

- *What would be an effective way to measure my success here?*

- *I'm curious to understand what drew you to the organization and what keeps you here.*

- *What separates this company from your competition?*

- *What is a possible career track for a successful employee here?*

Unfortunately, many interviewees will only inquire about benefits, vacation time, and work schedules. Never ask for details about these topics until you are under serious consideration for the position. The human resources representative or the hiring manager will most likely give you this information in writing later. By asking these questions early on, you are sending a message that you are more concerned about yourself than the company. An employer may also begin to question your work ethic and believe that you are more concerned with what the company has to offer you rather than what you have to offer to the company.

AVOID BUZZ WORDS

Another common mistake I witness all the time is the overuse of cliché buzz words. These are short phrases or descriptions such as people person, hard worker, fair, consistent. Job applicants say them repeatedly because they believe employers are looking for those qualities. Those descriptions have been so widely used, many people believe saying those phrases will boost their credibility. But if you don't have a story or details to back up a description of yourself, you will lose your credibility in the interview.

Employers will quickly lose interest when buzz words come out of your mouth without supporting evidence. Typically, job applicants will use these buzz words as a crutch. In reality, the clichés are meaningless. They make you appear as if you didn't know how to prepare for the interview, so you took the easy way out and spoke generally. You'll appear dull and blend in with all the rest of the candidates who used the same buzz words. Overly used phrases like "quick learner" do not paint a picture of who you are and what you bring to the table. All they do is fill in the gaps of the conversation and reveal your inability to truly communicate.

Employers have a picture of the ideal candidate. Buzz words are generic; they don't project unique characteristics.

Here's a quick exercise to demonstrate my point:

Think of your definition of a "people person" and write it down. Is this the same exact definition the person interviewing you has of this description? Of course not. Everyone's idea is different. A people person to you may be a caring, conscientious, bubbly, and outgoing person. But to the employer, "people person" could be the same type of person she just fired for spending more time socializing than doing his job.

Let's examine some other examples of statements that could be misinterpreted by your interviewer:

Poor statement: *I have a 4.0 GPA and am extremely proud of it.*

Employer thinks: *Oh great, a geek. He may be booksmart but does he have common sense? Can he function in the real world?*

Better statement: *I did very well in my classes, and they actually sparked my interest in this field.* (Let them know you before they know your GPA.)

Poor statement: *I'm extremely punctual.*

Employer thinks: *Let me guess—you're one of those people who clock in at 7:59 a.m. and you're the first one waiting by the time clock at 4:59 p.m., ready to check out.*

Better statement: *I hate to make people wait for me, so I always show up on time. My colleagues rely on me to be available at the same time every day, and I take that very seriously.*

Poor statement: *People really loved working for me in my last job.*

Employer thinks: *Ah, I know her type. Loves to be the cool, laidback boss and everyone's friend. It's more important for her to be liked than to do the job.*

Better statement: *If you asked the team I managed in my previous job about me, they'd tell you I was flexible whenever possible, but always held them accountable. I'm definitely not a micromanager.*

Poor statement: *I'm a hard worker. I'm not afraid to roll up my sleeves and get my hands dirty.*

Employer thinks: *Ten people have said that to me today. The last person I hired who said this was a recent college grad and he did just enough to get by at this place. Do these kids have any idea what hard work really is?*

Better statement: *I'm driven. My former boss told me I was his go-to person for the most difficult projects because he knew I would give every project my all. In fact, I got to know the janitor well because I spent many nights and weekends at the office.*

CHAPTER 7
PUTTING A TWIST ON HOW TO CLOSE THE INTERVIEW

There are enough guidebooks out there on how to close a job interview to fill up a small library. Some tell you to promise the employer you can start right away. Others tell you to leave a lasting impression with the perfect handshake. Unfortunately, I think many guides, though well-intentioned, fail to provide you with the appropriate ammunition to get the job.

I don't disagree with the traditional advice on how to close the interview. Of course, always be polite and thank the interviewer for taking the time to meet with you. Tell the employer you're interested in joining the organization and why. And don't shake your interviewer's hand like a limp fish or a bone crusher. But these aren't enough to secure what you set out for at the beginning of this process: the job.

So what else should you do? What is the big secret that libraries of employment guides have been unable to divulge? Well, it's not rocket science. But it is bold. After completing the interview, when the interviewer asks if you have any questions, ask this:

What makes me right and what makes me wrong for this job?

A good interview is an exchange of information from both the interviewer and the interviewee. Finding the information necessary to make a good hiring decision is very important to an employer, but it is just as important for you to obtain the information you need to decide whether or not to join a company. If you believe this is the job for you, wouldn't you like to know if the interviewer agrees with you?

As a lifelong Midwesterner, I can attest that I see lots of job candidates around here who are absolute pros at passive-aggressive "niceness." They want the job, but they don't want to appear pushy, confrontational, impatient, or unreasonable. They want to make the sale. But they've somehow picked up the lesson that the best way to get something is to sit patiently in the proverbial waiting room by the complimentary mints and *Field & Stream* magazines for someone to call their names. These candidates desperately want to know their chances of getting the job, but short of bugging the office or hiring a team of hackers to infiltrate HR's e-mail, they don't know how to get this information.

If you want to know where you stand, ask! When the interview is coming to an end and the employer asks if you have additional questions, there is your opportunity to find out where you stand.

Rather than smiling politely and wondering if you got the job, say this: *I have enjoyed our conversation, and I want to thank you for the opportunity to interview with your organization. I'm impressed with* _____. [1] *Quite frankly, I am extremely interested in becoming a member of your team. Now that you have learned more about me, from your perspective, what makes me right and what makes me wrong for this opportunity?*

---

1   Fill in the blank here with something substantive and honest, not "your office plants and the quick commute from my girlfriend's apartment."

From there, stop talking. Listen closely. Don't interrupt until the employer has finished completely. The typical response will be direct because the question is worded so precisely that it leaves no wiggle room. They will be inclined to give you feedback. Yes, they may tell you that they need to interview other candidates, before they make their decision. Whatever they say is better than nothing. Be prepared to hear, "Great portfolio, but not enough years of experience for us." Or, "We'd like to hire you, but we're worried about a conversation we had with your former employer." Whatever feedback your interviewer offers, receive it gracefully with appreciation. This information will help you.

If the interviewer explains that you are not a good fit for the company, you can respond in one of two ways:

1) You can work to overcome the objection. In other words, you can start with something along the lines of, "I'd like to take another stab at clarifying myself," or

2) You can find out where you are falling short, so that you work out those areas before interviewing with another employer. Think of it as free reconnaissance.

Remember, the reason for an interview is to exchange information, thereby allowing both sides to determine if each is right for the other. This way, you're not left to wonder if it's them or you.

The Salesman Who Saved Himself by Asking the Question

I once arranged an interview for a sales position requiring some travel. At the end of the interview, the candidate—we'll call him Ernie—followed my advice and asked, "What makes me right and what makes me wrong for this job?" The employer—we'll call him Gus—commented on how unfortunate it was that he wouldn't be able to hire Ernie, especially since his skill set and prior client base made him a perfect match for the organization. If only Ernie were willing to travel, Gus explained, he would hire him on the spot. Confused, Ernie then asked how much travel Gus anticipated, to which Gus answered, "two nights a week." Ernie sighed with relief and explained that in his current job, he was traveling five nights per week and hoping to cut it to three. With that, Gus smiled and asked when Ernie would be able to start.

Had Ernie never asked the question, both sides would have left the interview disappointed out of sheer miscommunication. It is crucial to know exactly where you stand.

On the same note, it's also important to accept the feedback—both positive and negative—with a good attitude. I've heard stories about candidates asking for feedback at the end of the interview and then aggressively defending themselves upon hearing the reasons why they weren't going to be hired. Keep your perspective in check. Use the input from the interviewer as a learning experience for future interviews. Consider it free advice from a person in the know! No matter what, maintain your professionalism and graciousness, and you'll be able to walk out of there with your head held high.

CONCLUSION
I BELIEVE IN YOU!

Let me tell you about the job interview that changed my life. It was 1977 and I was twenty-three years old, trying out for my first professional job as a loan representative. At that point, I had no college degree and no experience handling money. I had only held part-time jobs working for the YMCA and driving a laundry truck. (Those jobs paid $1.30 an hour if you can believe it.) Imagine me, sitting in the hot seat in the brand new J.C. Penney suit I bought specifically for that interview. (The suit certainly wasn't a fashion statement, but it showed my desire to be professional.) My friends had thought it was a waste of time because I was grossly inexperienced.

During the interview, the regional vice president asked me why he should hire me. I told him about my upbringing on a Minnesota farm and how my father had instilled in me an incredibly strong work ethic. I also illustrated my competitive spirit by telling him I had played in my high school basketball team for three years despite being the shortest guy on the team. I explained that I wasn't a naturally gifted athlete, but I outhustled everybody else and loved the thrill of working together to win.

By some miracle, I managed to get the job. Within a year of joining the financial institution I was promoted to branch manager, assigned to supervise several employees, and was the youngest employee to ever hold that position. Pretty good for a guy who had never managed anybody before that! That job was just the beginning for me. I picked up so many new skills that opened up more professional opportunities soon after.

So how did a farm kid, still wet behind the ears, manage to win over that regional vice president? My interviewer later explained that he was impressed by my energy, authenticity, and determination to win—regardless of the odds against me. And for him, those attributes made all the difference.

Times have certainly changed since 1977, but the purpose of the job interview remains the same. Employers are looking for people who can win them over with their energy, commitment, and passion. I wrote this book to show you how to win them over. Trust me, if I was able to do it, you can certainly do it.

Many of life's challenges can be overcome by starting with baby steps. I believe the interview process is no exception. When I set out to write this book, my intention was to offer everything I have learned over the last twenty years to help people, especially recent graduates who are facing an inordinately rough job market. I hope that this book helps you by eliminating your anxiety, building your confidence, and clearing up any misconceptions about job interviews.

Interviews can be scary for anyone, including the most seasoned professionals. But by sticking to the principles in this book, I guarantee that you will get better at job interviews. I believe in you!

Here are the five principles I want you to remember:

Employers want to see your heart and passion.

Stories are more powerful than facts. (Facts tell, but stories sell.)

Clarity is key. Make them understand. Don't make them guess.

Personality and professionalism outweigh skills.

The interviewer is the most important person on the face of the planet.

As I said earlier, this book was born out of my desire to help job seekers like you. I want every reader to benefit significantly from the career development materials we produce through Directional Motivation. Therefore, I have a personal request: I would like your feedback. If you feel that you have benefitted from something you have read and applied from this book, please contact me through my website at www.directionalmotivation.com and tell me about your experience. Also, feel free to recommend this book to friends that could benefit from it. I would be deeply honored in both cases.

Directional Motivation was founded specifically to help people improve their lives by providing career counseling and advice, books, live forums, videos, audio recordings, webinars, scholarships, apps, and other resources. We would love to help you. Visit us at www.directionalmotivation.com.

The little steps you take today
will determine your future success.

I wish you unlimited success. Go knock 'em dead!

REFERENCES

Alana Horowitz and Vivian Giang, "17 People Who Were Fired Before They Became Rich And Famous," *Business Insider*, March 31, 2012, accessed October 15, 2012, http://www.businessinsider. com/17-people-who-were-fired-before-they-became-rich-and-famous-2012-3?op=1#ixzz29RhxtIoI.

Amy Cuddy, "Your Body Language Shapes Who You Are," TEDGlobal 2012, Filmed Jun 2012, accessed March 4, 2013, http://www.ted.com/talks/amy_cuddy_your_body_language_shapes_who_you_are.html

Stephen Dubner, "The Upside of Quitting," Freakonomics Radio Podcast, Season 1, Episode 5, September 30, 2011, accessed October 15, 2012, http://www.freakonomics.com/2011/09/30/new-freakonomics-radio-podcast-the-upside-of-quitting/

FROM MY COLLECTION OF "WHAT WERE YOU THINKING?" STORIES

As I mentioned before, my life's purpose has been helping people. I love telling stories from my own experiences, particularly if there is a chance that even one snippet will make a meaningful difference in someone's life. I also mentioned that I love to make people laugh. So if I can leave you with three last tips of advice using real life anecdotes that might make you chuckle, I will be satisfied.

Absolute last tip No. 1: The impression you give to the employer starts from the first point of contact, including the moment you answer the phone. Unfortunately, I encounter a lot of job applicants with the worst phone etiquette. Here's an example of what I go through:

Russ: *Good Morning, my name is Russ Hovendick and I'm calling about the resume I received. Is this Neil Florem?*

Neil: *Ya, whatta ya want?*

Russ: *Actually Neil, I really don't want a thing. Sorry to have bothered you.*

Absolute last tip No. 2: E-mail addresses are not like tattoos. They can be changed.

Those wonderfully—how should I say—creative or personality-inspired e-mail addresses such as gangstawoman911@provider.com, bigstud1980@provider.com, disgirlsgotgame143@provider.com, killingmachine187@provider.com, or goodoleboy99@provider.net [2] don't portray you in the best light. Do you really think a recruiter or potential employer would consider it fun and quirky and want to

---

2   I'm not making these up. These are all based on real e-mail addresses we have seen on resumes. To protect the e-mail addresses, we have added numbers and left out the real e-mail providers.

contact you about a job opportunity? Quite the contrary. Whenever I see a resume with an e-mail address like this, I delete it immediately. There are plenty of other ways to express yourself. Keep your e-mail address simple and straightforward based on your legal name.

Absolute last tip No. 3: Know what the company does.

Research and practice take time, I know. But you have absolutely no excuse for coming to a job interview without knowing the company's products or services. Let this be the very first fact you find about a potential employer. If you show up clueless about the nature of the company, not only will you blow your chances of getting hired—you will give the person that rejected you a funny story to tell others.

This is a true story:

An applicant walks into a job interview for a quality supervisor position. After a few minutes into the interview, she asks, "Hey, what is it you guys make again?"

"We make beer," says the interviewer from the beer manufacturing company.

"Oh wow, I don't know if I could work for your company. I don't believe in alcohol consumption," she replies.

And that was the end of the interview. Even though I myself am not a consumer of alcohol, there is a lesson for everyone: always know the company's products or services before setting foot in a job interview.

ABOUT THE AUTHOR

Russ Hovendick is a national award winning executive recruiter. For twenty years, he has motivated hundreds of people through his multiple roles as recruiter, career coach, training consultant, business owner, and volunteer chaplain/counselor within the juvenile, jail, and prison system of South Dakota.

He heads Client Staffing Solutions, Inc., an executive recruiting agency, and recently founded the Directional Motivation Group www.directionalmotivation.com which offers career development books, training, webinars, scholarships, veteran services, career and life coaching, and other resources dedicated to making a difference in people's lives. With his positive approach and energetic personality, he is a frequent guest on radio and TV stations. His Directional Motivation book series has been widely endorsed by business and educational leaders across the country.

For booking inquiries, you may contact Russ at
russ@directionalmotivation.com.

Failed Interview questions will be a thing of the past!

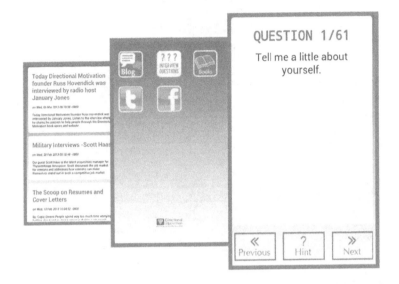

The new **Impact Interviewing App** from Directional Motivation provides you with the questions that employers are asking in today's competitive marketplace. Download this app from the GooglePlay Store Today!

CPSIA information can be obtained
at www.ICGtesting.com
Printed in the USA
BVHW040300050919
557639BV00002B/151/P